I HAVE NO IDEA
WHAT I'M DOING

POEMS ON PREGNANCY AND MOTHERHOOD

ILLUSTRATED BY ALLEGRA PILKINGTON

GRACE PILKINGTON

Quadrant Books

Quadrant Books

First published in 2021 by Quadrant Books
A member of the Memoirs Group
Suite 2, Top Floor, 7 Dyer Street, Cirencester, Gloucestershire, GL7 2PF

I HAVE NO IDEA WHAT I'M DOING
Paperback ISBN 978-1-7398645-1-4

Cover illustration by Allegra Pilkington

Typeset by Ray Lipscombe, Cirencester
Printed and bound in Great Britain

For my darling Alf - I'm sorry but it's true: I have no idea what I'm doing, but I'm trying and I love you.

And for Fred - Thank you. You're it.

Dear Little One

(Two Months, One Week Pregnant)

Dear Little One Growing Inside,

what's it like?

I haven't felt you move yet,

and sometimes, for a moment,

I forget.

Do you have enough food?

Is there anything I can do

to make it more

comfortable for you?

I wish you could talk to me,

tell me what you like

and what you don't like,

I wish you could tell me –

Hey, I'm alright

I wake every morning terrified

that you're no longer growing inside,

or that all the doctors

and scans lied,

and how I've cried,

thinking you're no longer growing inside.

Little one, do you feel that I'm scared

that I might not be good enough for you,

that I might fail you without meaning to?

I'm not always on top of things Little One,

I have a mind that is sometimes unkind,

it plays tricks on me and can make me blind

to all that's good, but I'll come back little one.

And never think I've gone there because of you,

and when I'm there, please remember it's all fake,

it's just a horrid dream, it will end and I will wake.

I love you with every cell of my being and that's what's real,

and unconditional love is all I want you to feel.

I hope I don't pass this on to you, I hope of its grasp
you'll be free,

I hope you know you're extraordinary and can be
whoever you want to be.

Little One, I promise everything will be okay,

I love you and will tell you every single day.

Dear Little One Growing Inside,

what's it like?

I hope you're alright.

Candy Crush Guy
(Four Months Pregnant)

My *Baby on Board* badge is pinned to a prominent
position on my coat.

As I board the Jubilee, the priority seat is snapped
up by a speedy bloke.

He looks right at me, then my badge, bump and
quickly averts eyes to his phone,

which hums while colours ping across the screen.
So here is a man fully grown,

suited, booted, fortyish, playing Candy Crush and
not offering me his seat,

Does he not think it might be hard balancing this extra
weight on these feet?

Does he not think... *Hold up! Maybe I can play
Candy Crush standing up?*

*'cause imagine if it was my mum or my girlfriend
up the duff,*

maybe they'd be feeling pretty rough,

maybe they'd be finding pregnancy tough,

*maybe she doesn't want to swing around, because
maybe she's feeling sick,*

*maybe I am a selfish prick, taking up a priority
seat for my minuscule dick,*

maybe I've prioritised myself enough and it's

time to think about someone else,

maybe more important than my candy crush league,
is someone else's health,

but he just concentrates harder on his screen and
shuffles his feet.

I HATE HIS SHOES

He dares to mock me in moccasins?

That's it, I can't take any more –

I declare war,

I start rubbing my stomach,

face pained, I puff, sigh and make sounds of despair,

while staring at a patch on his head which used to be hair.

People start to look at him in disgust,

aghast by his refusal to move,

but he doesn't do a thing, he doesn't stir,

my eyes are now clouded by red blur.

A woman jumps up and offers her seat,

but it's *his* seat I want now.

I want to sit on the seat warm from his farts,

and fantasise about tearing his body apart.

I move my bump closer towards him,

shoving my *Baby on Board* badge in his face.

A sensible inner voice squeaks -

You'll be done for harassment, calm down Grace.

Well, that voice has never been loud enough,
and now the nausea is off,
my chest burns and I'm swaying,
PING PING goes his Candy Crush thing.
He seems completely unaware of the rage he has unleashed,
of the gastric reflux climax that is about to be reached.
Meanwhile his game is reaching its peak.
I am feeling faint and weak and just about to vomit
all over his phone, that'll shut up its little ping-ping tone,
and then all over his smug little face.
The colourful fruits on his screen soon replaced
with real pieces of food,
last seen on yesterday's dinner plate,
but suddenly I hear an automated:
This is Warren Street.
I have to accept defeat,
he won, I didn't get my seat.
But that man is out there,
crushing candy as we speak,
and in five months time,
I'll find him and go into labour
on his moccasinned feet.

Warrior
(Four Months, Two Weeks Pregnant)

Your mum is a warrior.
At night she paints dark circles
around her eyes,
her fists clenched
and muscles tight,
she prepares to fight
the night.

Your mum is a warrior.
From the shelter of a sheeted tent,
she spreads
starfish fingers across
her stomach
and rocks through
the night.

Your mum is a warrior.
Etched across her chest
are tattoos of thought-up
future events

where she might fail you,
their ink itching, burning through
the night.
Your mum is a warrior.
Beating fists against her body,
she charges into a battle
she created,
screaming the war cry
of her worry, which echoes through
the night.

Second Trimester Bliss
(Five Months, One Week Pregnant)

I don't think I'm very good at this.

I don't smugly touch my swelling belly, grinning with pride,

I only touch it because I'm desperate to feel he's inside.

I'm not luminous, I don't radiate or feel in touch with the earth,

I don't feel calm and embracing of the fact I'll soon give birth,

I'm not going to have a baby in a tree, pool or on my home floor,

I want to be so plied with drugs

that through the pain, I just snore,

I don't feel certain that he's happy hanging out in my womb,

I worry it's not cushioned. Is there enough room?

I don't wake up feeling refreshed and ready for the day,

I feel terrified of everything that's to come my way,

I'm far too wrapped in a web of anxiety,

to talk about pregnancy with any piety.

No, I don't think I am very good at this,

I'm a far cry from Second Trimester Bliss.

Burping on the Tube
(Seven Months Pregnant)

I can't believe I have to do this,
I can't believe I have to do this
is all that's going through my head.
There's only one place I should be – bed.
Nobody told me about the crying,
nobody told me about the crying,
but here I am, floods of tears pouring from my eyes.
From the depths of my stomach, I feel vomit rise.
But it doesn't come.
I. wish. it. would
burp,
burp,
burp,
just another burp.
Burping and crying, I descend the escalator to the tube,
I walk painfully slowly, depressed and subdued,
I've just burped in a man's ear.
He looks round, horrified.
I want to rage – *have you ever had something growing inside ?*
Have you ever even tried?

No.

I thought not.

So let me burp.

I scowl at him.

He pulls out his phone.

Texting a friend?

Texting a friend, are you?

Really? Underground?

Is it actually going to go through?

What are you going to say?

That there's a mad, crying, burping woman

following you?

I sit opposite him on the carriage,

he's suited, middle-aged,

with a face annoyingly clean shaved

and for some reason,

to me, he has become

the Face of the Patriarchy.

I am staring at him, weeping,

snot dripping out my nose,

burping every minute or so.
He looks scared.

Actually,

he's looking at me

like I'm pathetic.

The patronising prick.

I bet he's called Simon

Or Paul

Or Patrick

I bet he cheats on his wife,

and to his kids, I bet he's not that nice

I bet he talks about money all the time,

I bet he bangs on about red wine,

I bet he doesn't understand a woman -

not *really*,

I bet he's never made one come.

I bet he wasn't there when his wife gave birth.

And suddenly I realise I am off the Tube,

following him down the street,

my footsteps quickening, pacing behind,

as I think of all the things he signifies.

He turns around and I hide behind a bin,

I can't even remember – how did this all begin?

But. I. can't. stop. following. him.

Now he has reached a gate -

Oh a front garden – lahdibloodydah!

He goes through it, towards the door,

which he unlocks and walks in,

and *damn* the curtains are closed,

I can't see in –

well, I guess that's it.

Whatever *it* is?

But shit, I really need to piss,

I don't suppose they'll notice,

if I just pull my pants down here,

Oh yes clean cut man – danger, danger, danger,

I am pissing all over your hydrangeas.

And suddenly the curtains are open

and his whole family can see,

me, in their garden,

having a pee.

He opens the window,

Get out! Get out! What's wrong with you?

I pull up my pants and trousers and run out the gate,

and I just can't remember the reason for all that hate,

but I think we can assume the lesson to be:

If I burp in your ear, smile,

nod in appreciation, even say *why thank you.*

Because there's no telling what a woman,

Seven months pregnant, might do.

Wow! This Sucks
(Seven Months, Two Weeks Pregnant)

I'm spitting with rage, an animal caged,

in a body and mind I don't recognise.

What about the glowing - was that all lies?

I used to love my husband, to adore every word he said,

now I'm so irritated by him, I question why he's in my bed.

He seems to always be there, always in my way,

making me a cup of tea or asking about my day,

How dare he?

How can I raise a child with him?

The whirring familiar doubts begin,

I despise everyone. Were they all just put on earth

to see who could be most annoying in my face first?

I feel hormones chugging through me, clouding my head.

My boobs ache and itch and my body longs to be in bed.

I no longer have thoughts. My head's filled with white noise,

I have lost all interests. I can't remember what Grace enjoys.

She's just some chick with a tendency to burp and drool,

some woman who's short tempered, snappy and cruel.

She seems determined to become as she feels -

isolated and disconnected,

Now? Really? Now?

I can't help but feel this is far from evolution perfected.

This is surely the time when I should be charming to all my dearest close and near,

so I have support when the little one hits the world and I'm overcome with fear.

So to all those mums out there who feel the same way,

but because of societal pressures don't feel it's okay to say:

You are not alone.

You can love the baby in your stomach very much,

and still find that pregnancy really, really sucks.

On the Verve

(Nine Months Pregnant)

Now the Gaviscon don't work,
it also makes you burp...
Lunch - I know I'll get that taste again,
Yeah, I know I'll get that taste again.

ALF IS BORN...

My Son Discovered His Hand
(Two Months, Three Weeks Old)

My son discovered his hand this morning,

it's not like it wasn't there before.

It was.

Hitting him in the face while he slept,

it kept poking his eye,

a fleshy spider in the way and he didn't know why.

Swaddled in a straight jacket we tried to contain it,

to restrain it,

from reflexes that perplexed

but this morning he discovered it.

He realised it was his,

attached to his body.

His.

His to control.

He pushes it through the space in front of him.

A miniature superman, tearing through blue skies.

His eyes watch it with wonder,

amazement.

Tightly clenched as if clutching sequins that have spilt

on the floor,

he spins it in the air,

opening it occasionally to reveal his shiny new palm.

He looks at his cocktail sausage fingers in awe,

his eyes are alight with admiration

for this new plaything he has found,

aglow with possibility, power.

My son discovered his hand this morning.

He was mesmerised by its grip.

If only we all looked at our hands in the same way,

each day,

as if we've just discovered them,

as if they've just appeared,

thinking carefully about what to do with them next.

I Thought That Was Tiring...

(Four Months Old)

I thought being a teenager was tiring.

Angsty, in tiny panties, snogging in pantries,

pay-as-you-go phone on loan from Mum

and mouth full of Hullabaloo bubble gum.

Cheap perfume, Charlie deodorant, *Mizz*, *Cosmo*,

staring at armpits, waiting for the occasional hair to grow.

Smoking Marlboro without inhaling,

attempting school exams and failing.

Angry diary entries and dramatic love letters

to teenage boys interested only in weed and the odd
computer game,

each week the declaration of love addressed to a
different lad's name.

Disappointment and depression on the rejection
of each confession,

then the desperate suppression of feelings.

Hours spent sleepless, staring at ceilings.

Absurdly self-obsessed, crushingly insecure,

The constant feeling that I couldn't take any more.

I thought *that* was tiring.

I thought my first job was tiring.

After three lazy years at uni,

I was tied to a desk, desperate for approval.

Eager to please and terrified of reproval.

Stuck in the web of lies formed in my CV disguise,

GCSE French forged as fluency.

Late nights in the office quickly turned

to later nights spending cash newly earned,

chasing around my first love – he was older and angry —

trying to prove I was rageful and worthy.

Candle burning at all ends, seeking scurvy.

Mac and cheese for lunch

and an afternoon Apple Mac pass-out

when nobody was about.

Stinking of booze, dehydrated and fixated on bed,

but on leaving the office, going for a *few* drinks instead.

A vicious circle of contortion and exhaustion,

ignoring all bodily signs to take caution.

I thought *that* was tiring.

Feeding, burping, jiggling, playing,

watching every move and swaying,

panicked, anxious or in utter bliss,

Googling – What's that? What's this?

Up, down, up, up, and down again,

take a deep breath and count to ten

2am, 4am, 6am and then awake –

that's it, the night has gone.

The day is even more full-on.

Nappy change, breast, nappy change, breast,

or unable to move as someone's sleeping on my chest.

All plans out the window, going nowhere fast,

leaving the house now the most momentous task,

high on adrenalin and purpose

or tearful, scared and morose.

If not feeding or assisting in napping and crapping,

I'm in a state, marching about and flapping.

I have no control over time, it's not something I own,

and nor are my arms, *'they're too weak'* I moan,

as they get caught in awkward positions and go dead from weight.

I arrive at everything a milk-drenched zombie, horribly late.

He's either in a sling, attached to my boob or rocking in my arms,

while I try desperately to keep him happy and calm.

Dabbing my nipple as it squirts milk everywhere,

or trying to remove curdled spit up from my hair.

I spend hours staring at his minuscule hands and feet,

or bouncing on the spot to get him to sleep.

But one thing is for sure – I do not really sleep anymore.

My mouth is filled with ulcers and my eyes with styes,

and I realise all those times

I thought I was tired

from merely staying up late,

That wasn't anything at all.

I knew rest was coming. It only ever lasted a night or two,

And would eventually end in sleep – *that* I always knew.

No, I wasn't tired then.

Now I am tired,

Now I am tired.

Free to Thrash

(Four Months, Two Weeks Old)

Thrashing about

and screaming

legs kicking,

arms hitting

out at space

red, pained face,

eyes shut,

inconsolable.

How I long to

step inside your mind,

fiddle around without

making a sound.

I'd make everything okay and fair,

you'd never know I'd been in there;

I'd leave subtly -

quietly climb down a hair.

I'd take away all pain,

and if it had to go somewhere,

I'd swallow it,

GULP,

and feel my throat,

fizz and burn.

Oh! I yearn

to get a key

to that mind of yours.

When you came out of me,

I should've asked for one,

so I could find the cause of this pain,

but this seems to be the thing

about the motherhood game

that will turn me insane:

the constant swinging

between two modes of

thinking -

Ahh help! The responsibility is too much

to

Am I doing enough? Is there more I can do?

or

Oh! how I want to be inside your brain

to

Oh! how wonderful it is watching you be you.

I guess it's lucky they

didn't give me a key,

because what an intruder

I'd be.

You should be free

to thrash around,

to scream and wail,

and all I can do is try

and most probably

fail

to make you feel better.

Henry the Hoover

(Five Months, One week old)

He moved in after Christmas.
You watched him make himself at home
under the stairs,
snuggled up
next to a bag containing
his many heads.
Whenever we'd pass his campsite,
I'd feel you tense,
your fists clench,
as you'd look at him,
half hoping he'd still be there,
half hoping he'd be gone.
When I first got him out,
your eyes
wide and terrified,
unblinking.
I switched him on, and as his black trunk
skimmed the floor, you screamed,
your bottom lip rolled over,
a pink carpet coming undone,

chin quivering,

I turned him off.

After that, I'd use him

when you were asleep.

But you kept looking for him.

One morning you reached

out and shook his hand.

Now when he starts to purr,

you follow him in awe,

you paw his shiny red suit,

as if an exciting new fruit.

You look to him for lessons on

how to be,

and lucky me to get to see,

how quickly fear of something unknown

can transform into admiration full blown.

Mum's Net

(Five Months, Three Weeks Old)

I'm stuck in a mum's net,

I was just having a dip,

I got worried about something

I can't remember what...

Why won't baby sleep in his cot?

Or maybe, *why is baby pulling on his ears?*

Or *what does it mean if crying without tears?*

I can't even remember what.

I got worried about something,

I was just having a dip.

I'm stuck in a mum's net.

Mum-station: Darling D (daughter) did exactly this when she was 2 months old,

No.1mum: probably because she was teething/hungry/overtired or really cold.

Naturalmamma: DH (husband) thought she was hot and put ice down her front,

Hardmummy: Naturalmamma you should ditch your DH, he sounds like a c***

I'm stuck in a mum's net.

I was just having a dip.

I got worried about something.

I can't remember what.

(Message withdrawn at administrator's request)

Supermum and Me

(Six Months Old)

'Six months! How's the night? Sleeping through, right?'

asks yet another well-slept and slightly smug mother.

STUDY MY FACE

Are these eyes open and bright or bagged and tight?

Do they really look like they've been closed all night?

They haven't just returned with a tan from a luxurious holiday on the Isle of Nod,

They're more hiking boots, backpack on, torch out – survival mode, praying to God.

This mouth is too tired to answer, but it lets out a *'Ha! If only!'*

I am now hallucinating that she is the pink one from My Little Pony,

with her brushed, shiny hair, wide mascaraed eyes and smooth moisturised skin,

'James was definitely sleeping through the night by then and so were the twins!'

I am now staring into space, dribbling from exhaustion,

caution, caution,

I am about to pass out all over your quilt of bullshit,

it looks so comfortable, feathery, soft and oooh is it silk?

Three babies sleeping all night long, not interested in milk?

No teething, no regression, no babbling, no crying?

Just every night seven till seven – PLEASE tell me you're lying.

You rummage through your colour-coordinated nappy bag,

everything neatly placed and very tightly packed,

different compartments for sweet and savoury snacks.

I bet your kitchen is labelled and you ALWAYS wear matching socks.

My bag spills onto the floor – dirty muslins, dummies fly out their box.

I start to pick things up and notice, while down there, a slight smell of dog poo.

If I was to lift my foot, I know I'd find it squidged into the grooves of my shoe.

Supermum picks up a nappy *'Are you okay there, can I give you a hand?'*

I stare at her skin tone against the Pamper's green. HOW is she so tanned?

I watch her moisturised nose twitch, mine still flakey from last month's snuffle,

Oh no she can smell it! She thinks it's me! *'Thank you!'* I say, *'Such a kerfuffle!'*

A wail comes from the pram,

Alf! You beautiful little man!

'Thank you for your help! I think he's hungry so I better go'

'No worries! Nice to meet you! I hope you get some rest'

I walk away, knowing I've failed the efficient parenting test.

But I don't frown, wail or cry,

only let out a self-accepting sigh.

I pick up my foot and as expected, there's shit all over the sole,

I look at you, a smile twitches across you, eating your face whole,

I was always under-slept, odd socks, broken bag and shitty shoe,

it's really nothing new.

But now I get to be all those things AND hang out with you.

That's a Funny Sound for the Sea to Make

(Seven Months, One Week Old)

I awake abruptly,

as if I've never been to sleep,

eyes peeled.

It's 2am.

He will wake. any. second. now.

Nothing.

Any second now

I will hear a squeak.

Nothing.

Which will turn to a cry,

a wail.

Any second now.

Nothing.

The cot is still.

What's he doing in there?

Sleeping?

It can't be so!

I look at my phone –

it has been four hours

WOAH!

Perhaps I have a baby who sleeps through the night?

I put all the nights,

him in my arms,

eyes open wide,

aside and

feel my body heat with pride.

I feel glowing and light

but, actually,

this is unlike him.

I hope he's alright?

With a hand on the little chest I adore,

I feel it rise and am assured.

So where was I?

Lying in bed,

resting my head,

the head of a mother whose child sleeps through the night!

I start to imagine a life well slept, rested,

waking up feeling refreshed,

the grog lifting,

tired blur shifting.

It'll give a reset to my brain,

I'll start to feel sane—

REFRAIN from getting ahead of yourself—

he will wake up.

Any

second

now.

Wait, wait, wait–

what am I still doing awake?

I should be asleep!

'Sleep when your baby sleeps' they say.

But I can't seem to nap in the day,

SO I MUST SLEEP NOW

Deep breaths,

think of the waves

crashing on the shingle,

breath in and out,

in and...

Oh no! A thought is in my way:

What should I cook for tomorrow's lunch?

What do we have left in the fridge?

Hmmm that bacon needs to be munched,

and we should probably eat that cheese,

perhaps I'll get the dal out the deep freeze

Wait, is this necessary?

NO

Go to sleep, go to sleep, go to sleep,

Remember when you were seventeen

and you had a cigarette with Juad out the window?

NO!

That's completely irrelevant, it's not even an interesting memory,

Really! If you're going to go through EVERY single thing you're going to be up all night

and exhausted from thinking such pointless stuff,

but I wonder if we should get some new curtains?

ENOUGH ENOUGH

How can you expect him to sleep after 9 months here,

when you haven't cracked it and it's your 32nd year!

He will be awake soon and the day will start—

Back to the waves crashing on the shingle,

In, out. In, out.

WAHHHH

Oooh that's a strange sound for the sea to make...

That's not the sea.

That's him.

He's awake.

Human Being

(Seven Months, Three Weeks Old)

Have you tried white noise?

Or what about brown noise?

Or one of those owl toys?

Singing?

What with my voice?

I think not

I hear that helps a lot...

Book before bed?

Stroking his head?

Same time every night, you say?

Could it be teeth getting in the way?

Hmmm...

I don't know what else to say.

What do you think it is?

Mother's instinct knows.

Or other mother's instincts know—

have a look on Mumsnet

Try some Calpol

See how it goes...

Difference between day and night –

he knows that, right?

Can he self-settle?

Self-soothe?

What do you think it is?

Mother's instinct knows.

Separation anxiety?

Too hot?

Too cold?

The truth is nobody has any clue.

Well, my darling, apart from you.

You are your own little man,

a human being,

not a piece of machinery

with a flashing light:

STILL HUNGRY

COLD

FRONT TOOTH HURTS

So it's all guesswork, what happens at night,

but I'll keep guessing, hoping I get it right.

Truth is I've never been good at getting myself to sleep,

if I were a machine, there'd be a question-mark bleep,

BEEP BEEP BEEP going off almost every eve.

I'm not sure what happens with my mind and body,

so I'll not claim to know what happens in yours,

but I'll learn who you are, what helps, what you like best,

and will try my absolute hardest to help you get some rest.

How Small You Are

(Eight Months, Three Weeks Old)

It was completely bizarre,

for a while I forgot

how small you are.

You were so busy,

clambering around with

pots and pans,

stirring and slaving

over nothing.

Using everything as a drum,

sniffing out fluff and crumbs

on the floor -

things at lunch

you'd chosen to ignore.

You'd sit opposite me

munching

your cucumber stick

talking literature

and politics,

what Donaldson

you're reading

and what toy

was up to what

in your play-pen cabinet

and so I guess that led me

to forget,

just for a while,

how small you are.

Then the temperature came,

the screaming in pain,

refusing to sit in your seat,

no interest in play-pen politics,

or the whereabouts of Spot,

refusing to sleep in your cot,

so it was back to

us.

Us in bed together,

both in pants

and vest,

you nibbling on my breast.

Again you were tiny,

minuscule,

attached,

nuzzled into my skin.

And for a second,

I did let out a grin.

Through all the

anxiety and

longing for you

to feel okay,

it felt special

to lie around

cuddling all day.

Back at Work

(Nine Months, One Week Old)

Yes, I completely agree, the figures are in the nappy bag—

Oh sorry did I say nappy bag? Baby Brain - isn't that sad?

Let me email you over some puree this afternoon—

Oh sorry did I say puree? You must think I'm a loon!

Let me just take a look at my dummy and get back to you—

Oh sorry did I say dummy? I've lost it - what am I to do?

Attached here. I look forward to hearing your sippy cup—

Oh sorry, did I just say sippy cup? I'm a complete nut.

Great! And do you think you can have that for me by muslin?

Oh sorry, did I say muslin? Your patience must be wearing thin -

It is?

Well yes, I suppose you can tell

I'm not juggling things too well

My apologies,

I really am so sorry.

Try and be understanding. Try to be fair,

I did this conference call whilst cleaning a highchair.

And actually screw you, I'm not sorry, I'm not.

I wrote this email with one hand in a cot.

Dinner-time

(Nine Months, Two Weeks Old)

Head shaking,

table nearly breaking

thumping hand,

he tries to stand,

to lift himself

out of his seat

beating his feet

does he want less

or more?

I can't be sure.

Sort of crying,

sort of screaming

Hmm…

What's the meaning?

Desperate for more?

Or really not a fan?

A furious little man,

waving a crisp in

front of my nose,

temptingly close,

I feel my own
tummy rumble,
perhaps if
I just have
a litttttllleee
nibble, it will put
this quibble
to bed.
Mouth open,
I move towards
his tiny head,
'*Yumm!*'
I say exaggeratedly,
biting down
on his snack,
there's something
fleshy in my mouth,
Whats's that?
I see his lip shake
and tears form
in the corners of his
eyes,
As they plead
WHY?

And that's when I

realise,

I've bitten it.

His finger!

My darling son!

Just because

I was peckish

and thought it would

be fun.

Fuck! I'm a terrible mum,

I wrap him in my arms

tell him I never meant any harm,

Help!

I need to be rid of my greed –

I nearly made my son bleed!

I almost munched his finger

while he was trying to feed.

Lockdown

(Ten Months Old)

Let's do a recipe swap!
I've been cooking such a lot,
I've developed a recipe for a summer stew,
It uses up scraps - I'll send it to you...

I still haven't had time to shave my legs.

I've been doing such a lot of DIY,
I'm pretty good at it, not going to lie!
Let's discuss house and garden design,
Perhaps on Zoom over a glass of wine?

I still haven't had time to shave my legs.

I've just read *Anna Karenina* AND *War and Peace*,
and do daily nursery rhymes on FaceTime with my niece!
I'm also working on my memoir - yes, yes! I'm writing a book...
It just sort of came to me - don't suppose you could take a look?

I still haven't had time to shave my legs.

I've got to say I've become a real fitness queen,
It just makes me feel good - know what I mean?
And yoga! My cobra is so snaky, it's actually scary!
What did you say? Surely not. They can't be that hairy?

They are, they are.

I still haven't had time to shave my legs.

Leaving the House Without You

(Eleven Months Old)

I leave the house,

quickly.

I feel naked.

I look down,

I'm not.

A relief –

for the neighbours, mainly,

it wouldn't be fair.

Personally I'm not anti

a supermarket shop stripped bare,

but not sure Morrisons is ready

for my Covid pubic hair.

Did I forget my wallet?

In my bag,

I have a rummage,

no, it's there.

My keys?

Oh please,

let it not be my keys!

I hear their clink

Well, what?

Hmmm, let me think…

My phone!?

Nope. Got it!

I see you on my screen.

Ah!

I no longer stall,

I keep walking,

You're not with me,

that's all.

Desperately Domestic

(Eleven Months, One Week Old)

You have a set of dinosaurs, all brightly coloured,

but you prefer to rearrange the kitchen cupboard.

You have a set of neon magnets which coolly attach to metal,

but you prefer to garden, dead-heading every single petal.

You have a tambourine, a set of drums and a triangle too,

but you'd rather spend the day slaving over a leaf stew.

You have a vast innovation station with things to twirl, grab, activate and spin,

But you'd prefer to load the washing machine and twitch, waiting for it to begin.

You have a giant penguin the size of a small person,

but you'd prefer to hoover and smooth ruffled curtains.

How I long to tell you *Alf! You'll be doing this stuff for eternity,*

don't go all domestic now — ditch the broom and mop and roam free.

And if that fails, I'd love to give you a tip or two on how to get things really sparkling and clean,

So you could do the sweeping while I sit with a cup of milk and play with your music machine.

Fingers in the Plug Socket

(Eleven Months, Two Weeks Old)

I used to be a risk taker,

occasionally a rule breaker,

a sky-diver,

needing to be higher

and higher,

jumping bungee,

adrenalin junkie.

Always up for a paraglide,

or a speedy funfair ride,

unafraid of dying,

unafraid of heights,

sharks, lions, tigers,

I wasn't bothered,

no matter how big,

I would've had 'em

round for a cider and cig.

But then something happened.

I became a mum,

suddenly I shun

all risk taking, all rule breaking,

I want to be grounded,

REALLY grounded,

stuck to the earth.

It seems I hit the hard

adrenaline giving birth,

now I'm done with it,

over it.

I've had my fill,

turned my back on the thrill.

I'd rather go for a relaxing walk.

Maybe if I'm not too knackered,

I'll talk.

You won't see me spending hours at Alton Towers,

looking for rides to momentarily take my breath,

No — my flirtation with death died its own death,

and gone is the desire for a skydive.

I'm busy trying to keep someone alive.

Imagining I live on the floor,

with all its plugs and stairs,

gives me plenty of scares,

I don't need anything more.

Because things have never been more risky,

on a day to day, than making sure a tiny man is okay.

A Year Ago

(Twelve Months Old)

A year ago I was a whale, staggering from the sea,

the shingle stabbed and kneaded my feet,

As I thought - I guess this counts as reflexology?

I tucked into tupperware tight with pineapple,

spreading fingers over my ballooned middle,

Feeling for signs of you, your okayness, your arrival,

My mind had been awash with anxiety about your survival,

and now it was eleven days past the day they said you were due,

and for the first time in pregnancy, I felt calm spread through

my achey, sciatic body as I huffed and puffed up the hill.

We bumped into a stranger who, pointing at you, told us
drunkenly:

Yup, I had 3 of those and then I went for a vasectomy

We laughed, sweat filling follicles on my forehead,

I think, *when we get back, I'll have to go to bed*

But you had a different idea;

it was your time to appear,

my body started to contract,

as I tried to breathe through the agony

of you making your way out of me,

waters breaking whilst watching Peep Show,

us calling the hospital every hour or so,

until they said *'It's time to come in.'*

The next hours blurred by pain,

remnants of memories -

a mean midwife, Coca Cola,

Shut that up I screamed

when my labour playlist started to stream,

an intern giving a detailed audio guide of Dartford Park,

and wearing sunglasses,

even though it wasn't dark.

The midwives changed shift at 7am,

I heard their plans for the weekend

as your head started to crown.

I gave birth to you at 7.28am

Even at 7.28am, I was still that Grace,

deeply shocked and spaced.

But half an hour later everything changed—

I felt a love move within me that meant

every organ inside me had to be rearranged

to accommodate the wonder of you,

so much so, that saying 'Alf gave birth to Grace

at 7.58am' feels more true.

The Last Boob

(Thirteen Months Old)

I didn't realise it was going to be the last boob,

I hadn't been concentrating,

I didn't spend it watching you,

watching me.

I didn't spend it marvelling at the way my

boobs, never bigger than a B

provided your breakfast, elevenses, lunch

and tea,

and many a middle of the night snack,

until desperate sleep deprivation

put a stop to that.

I didn't realise it was going to be the last boob,

I wasn't concentrating,

I was reading the news,

I can't remember what,

but now if I could choose

between reading the news,

and watching you, watching my

body provide you with food,

I know what I'd choose.

I Want My Body Back

(Thirteen months, two weeks old)

I want my body back

I said.

I shared it with you for two years,

first it was your home,

and then essentially a restaurant,

I want my body back

I lied.

But I didn't get my body back -

larger and greener is my varicose vein,

my stomach is forever changed,

my breasts are sagging and unfull,

gravity has had a pull

on everything.

So it's not the same body,

it was hit by the most beautiful hurricane,

and can never be the same.

I'm now an empty vessel,

one which was full of you,

and as of late,

I sort of wish,

you'd never had to vacate.

I want to share my body with you,

any chance you still want that too?

Your First Day

(Fifteen Months Old)

You'll look back,
I think.
If I was holding a snack,
I think you'd look back,
but you walk on,
into the arms of a twenty-something
with a plastic shield over her face.
You're not smiling,
nor frowning
you're exploring
and ignoring
me,
who is standing behind you
saying
Alf, I love you, see you later!
I thought you'd look back
and see my face
momentarily attacked
by love for you
and misery at the fact,

that in a minute, if that,

I'll watch my

feet walk away.

But then I have my hand in his,

and we're pacing,

pram free,

towards the sea.

There's nobody,

just gulls,

splashing their faces

ready for

the morning ahead:

sleepy and

barely out of bed.

And for a moment,

it's just like before,

before you,

when we were just two.

Strangely alien,

strangely familiar.

We eat poached eggs

and fumble with papers,

it has been fifteen months,

since I've seen my

greasy fingerprint

against the

paper's grey,

but here it is,

today.

And you're there.

Are your hands pressed

against a wall?

As you walk on shaky

new legs and try not

to fall?

Are you looking back now?

Suddenly the App bleeps,

Telling us what you've had

to eat:

Cheerios, ate them all

Of course you did.

You're not looking back.

And I feel sick and elated,

that you can do it—

you can be,

in the world,

without me.

BV - #0080 - 300524 - C0 - 216/138/4 [6] - CB - 9781739864514 - Gloss Lamination